Clifford's Tower
and the Castle of York

Jonathan Clark

Introduction

Clifford's Tower was once the impressive keep of York Castle, sitting at the centre of a range of castle buildings. Perched on a motte presiding over the rivers Ouse and Foss, it still dominates the city of York, looking over to its sister motte, Baile Hill. Prompted by rebellions in the North, William the Conqueror erected these two mottes in the late 1060s. York Castle was a strategic stronghold in the North, serving as the backdrop for events of national and international significance. Most notorious was the attack on the Jewish community in 1190, when the Jews of York took refuge in the tower from a vicious pogrom and died in the most tragic circumstances.

During the reign of Henry III (r. 1216–72), the large stone tower, which we now know as Clifford's Tower, was constructed. The tower was later named after the Clifford family, who acted as constables of the castle in later years. One member of the family, Lord Roger de Clifford, was executed in 1322 and his body was hung in chains from the tower walls.

For much of the 14th and 15th centuries, Clifford's Tower was used as a treasury, exchequer, mint, gaol and seat of royal power. During the Civil War (1642–9), Clifford's Tower was held by the royalists while the city was under siege. In 1684 the tower was reduced to a shell after a fire. Eventually, most of the castle buildings were swept away when a new prison and court were built in the 18th and 19th centuries, leaving Clifford's Tower as an isolated relic of York Castle.

Above: *A wax impression of the 13th-century seal of the sheriff of Yorkshire, showing a castle with three towers*

Facing page: *The forebuilding of Clifford's Tower, parts of which date back to the 13th century*

Tour

Clifford's Tower is one of the main surviving medieval features of York Castle. Sadly, the building is now a shell. The tour begins on the ground floor, which at one time housed the royal exchequer and treasury. The first floor, which was used as private apartments, includes a richly decorated chapel. A wall-walk provides a panorama across the city of York and a good vantage point from which to appreciate the layout of the medieval castle. The tour also includes a walk round the other remains of the medieval castle.

FOLLOWING THE TOUR
The tour starts on the ground floor just by the ticket office. The numbers beside the headings highlight the key points on the tour and correspond with the small numbered plans in the margins.

■ FOREBUILDING

The ground floor of the forebuilding would have been used as a reception area; a stone bench along the east wall was used by those waiting to be admitted. Stairs on the west side of the entrance, added in the 17th century, provided access to floors and rooms above. A pointed doorway incorporating a portcullis slot, operated from above the gate passage, leads into the main tower.

Above the entrance are two shields. The upper one is of Charles I (r.1625–49), inserted in 1643 when the tower was reinforced during the Civil War. The one below bears the arms of Henry Clifford, 5th earl of Cumberland, who had been lord lieutenant of the northern parts and governor of York until his death in 1643. The Clifford family provided the tower with its name: Roger de Clifford was executed and hung from the tower in 1322, and later descendants acted as castle constables.

The north-eastern side of the forebuilding dates back to the 13th century, including the side of the door and part of the arch. A vertical scar in the wall next to the doorway marks the remains of one of two stone walls, which once flanked the original stairs going up to the tower. The majority of the south-east and south-west sides of the forebuilding date from the 17th century. The later sections are characterized by the use of a mauve-tinted sandstone and reused limestone.

GROUND FLOOR

Clifford's Tower is now just an empty shell, devoid of its upper floor, roof and internal walls. It is a challenge to visualize the layout of the interior, but originally the ground floor was divided into a number of separate rooms.

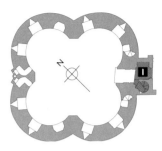

Below: The arms of Henry Clifford on the forebuilding. The Cliffords were hereditary constables of York Castle
Bottom: *The forebuilding and the south-east façade of the tower. Additional floors and a stair were added to the forebuilding when it was reconstructed in the 1640s*

Facing page: *The spiral stairs leading up to the first floor*

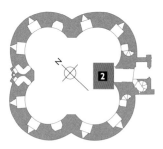

Facing page: This cutaway reconstruction shows the square structure within Clifford's Tower that appears in plans and views of the 1680s. Sir Christopher Musgrave made a detailed inventory of the contents of the tower in 1682, listing among other things, 16 guns, over 1,000 muskets and ammunition

Below: The arrangement of Clifford's Tower, with a central tower built within a 'shell' tower on a motte, may parallel that at Launceston Castle, shown here in this view of about 1770 by Hendrik Franz de Cort

Central Tower

There is much evidence to suggest that there was once an additional, central square tower, now vanished, which provided further rooms in the centre of the building. Seventeenth-century plans show that the square tower's corners were at the centre of each lobe, so they could have supported radial first-floor bridging beams in the lobes. Large blocked sockets in the walls indicate the position of the beams.

From 17th-century drawings we know that the central square tower was taller than the outer walls of Clifford's Tower; its roof served as a gun platform during and after the Civil War. Damaged by an explosion of gunpowder in 1684, the tower was cleared away in the early 18th century, leaving no visible trace. It is not clear when the square tower was built, but it might either have been a feature of the original design, or constructed during the Civil War.

Marked on the ground in the centre of the tower is the position of an octagonal stone pier, which supported the first floor in the 13th century. The pier was probably removed when the square inner tower was built.

2 Entrance Lobby

Immediately in front of the entrance arch was a room formed by timber partition walls on either side of the entrance and by the south-east wall of the central square tower. This room served as a lobby, with doorways leading off to rooms in the east and south lobes and the central tower.

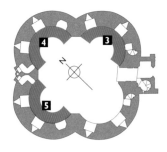

3 East Lobe

The east lobe, to the right of the entrance, housed part of the service area of the tower. The room contained a well, now covered with a grill, which we know from the exchequer accounts required repair in 1318. Natural light for the room came from the two deep window embrasures, each containing an arrow slit, which widens to a rectangular window above. A doorway next to the entrance leads to a spiral stair up to the first floor and wall-walk.

Large sockets in the stonework, level with the tops of the window embrasures and now filled with brick or rubble, originally contained corbels to support vertical timber posts. The posts supported the main beams of the first floor and, in some cases, extended higher to support the roof structure. There are many more sockets in the wall of the east lobe, in contrast to the other lobes. Subsidence of the tower, first recorded in the 14th century, resulted in the outward movement of the walls, which would have made many of the original floor beams too short for their span. Rather than removing the failed beams, the solution appears to have been to insert additional sockets and further beams to support the first floor.

4 5 North and West Lobes

The north and west lobes, opposite the entrance, each contain latrines and the only remaining fireplaces in the building. From 1298 some of the rooms in Clifford's Tower on occasion housed the exchequer and treasury, and there is some evidence to suggest they might have been in the north lobe. The medieval office of the exchequer managed and accounted for the royal revenue. The word 'exchequer' comes from a board or counter around which the accounts of each local sheriff were audited. The treasury, which was an office within the exchequer, collected and issued money. There is evidence for a timber screen, which would have been used in the exchequer: a socket in the wall of the north lobe between the

Above: One of two surviving fireplaces in Clifford's Tower, which might have been used to test the metal in coins
Right: A 15th-century illustration of the exchequer of Ireland at work. The squares on the table each stood for a value. The counters showed how much money was owed and the tally sticks recorded how much had been paid to the Crown. Clifford's Tower housed the exchequer from 1298

Medieval Coinage

The precise date for the establishment of a mint at the castle is unknown, but the mint is recorded as having been rebuilt in 1353 and again in 1423. The later rebuilding ties in with a record of a London goldsmith and master of the king's mint, Bartholomew Seman, being authorized to coin at York and Bristol in February 1423. Upon being sent to York he was 'to coin there the gold and silver of the said country that was not of right weight, and to remain there during the king's pleasure'. Bartholomew Seman, alias Goldbeter, was later appointed as master and worker of the 'mistery' of the king's mint within the castle in January 1424 until his death in about 1431.

Clearly there were problems with the existing buildings, because in April 1423 the mint, melting house, furnaces, treasury and house for the moneyer and servants were all rebuilt. Subsequently, Thomas Roderham was appointed to the post of controller, changer and assayer of the king's money within the castle of York and Thomas Haxby, clerk and treasurer to the cathedral, was appointed warden, receiver of the profits and keeper of the dies. Some of the buildings that were used by the mint were based elsewhere in the castle, but the actual assaying of the coins (checking their metal content) might have taken place in Clifford's Tower – a secure environment in which to handle the precious metals. The fireplaces in the tower appear to have been designed as hearths for the assaying process.

A London goldsmith, Bartholomew Seman, was authorized to coin at York in 1423 and was 'to remain there during the king's pleasure'

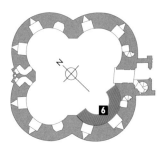

Below right: The interior of the north lobe. Some of the offices of the exchequer would have been housed in this part of the building

Facing page: An aerial view of Clifford's Tower with York Minster in the background. The area between Clifford's Tower and the church spire in the middle of the photograph would once have been occupied by the outer bailey, or courtyard, of the castle

'Prepare the tower with doors, bars and locks and other things which are lacking for the safeguarding of our treasury which we will place there, as John Dymmok, usher of our exchequer, shall more fully explain on our behalf.' Edward I, in a 13th-century manuscript, instructing the sheriff of York in 1298

fireplace and one of the window embrasures is at just the right height for a screen. Other items of furniture, listed in an inventory, included a large counter 13ft by 12ft (4m by 3.7m), made of fir boards bordered with oak, on which money would have been counted, with the oak border slightly raised to prevent the money falling off the table.

Both fireplaces have flues which taper to a very small size and the proportions of the fire openings are unusual: their heights are disproportionate to their widths. Such narrow flues are sometimes used in metalworking furnaces or hearths, where a fast 'draw' is required, and it is possible that the fireplaces were intended as hearths associated with minting and the assay of precious metals.

6 South Lobe

The south lobe has two window openings and a door to a spiral stair, which provides access to the chapel, first floor and wall-walk. The south lobe contained smaller rooms, which might have served as guard and service rooms. Sockets in the walls set at various heights reflect the position of internal partitions.

FIRST FLOOR

The first-floor rooms were designed to provide secure accommodation for the king and queen, but they were rarely used as such. Other important people, however, did stay in the tower, including the countess of Buchan and her children in 1338. Alice, countess of Buchan, was a member of a powerful Scottish family, but in 1310 she married Henry de Beaumont, later a key ally of Edward III in the wars against Scotland. One condition of her stay was 'that the king's things in the tower be safely kept for his use'. The first floor would have been subdivided, with the two spiral stairs on either side of the

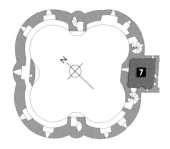

main entrance providing access to two separate suites of apartments. The south and east lobes each have a larger pointed window, lighting principal rooms. A partition would have run along the main line of symmetry (from north-west to south-east) and is indicated by the position of the small window into the chapel in the forebuilding, offset to one side of the partition line. Both apartments had direct access to the chapel, visually or physically, one via the small window and one directly from the spiral stair to the south lobe. This suggests that bedchambers would have been located in the south and east lobes, since access to a chapel at all times of the day was seen as essential in the Middle Ages.

Between the west and north lobes is a single latrine reached by doorways on either side, and shared between the two sets of apartments. Further doorways between the lobes to the east and west provided access to spiral stairs, contained within small turrets, leading to the wall-walk. It is likely that the floor was further subdivided from west to east, to form inner and outer chambers on either side of the tower. Any fireplaces have now vanished, but early illustrations show chimneys emerging from the centre of the tower. The first floor might also have housed the treasury first mentioned in 1298 in an order from Edward I to the sheriff of York.

7 Chapel

The first floor of the forebuilding contains the chapel, which is reached from the spiral stair in the south lobe. The chapel would once have been beautifully decorated. Sections of blind arcading survive, with pointed arches originally supported on slender shafts with moulded capitals and bases. The north-west wall has an aumbry, a cupboard for holy vessels, and above this a small window or squint. This would have provided a clear

Above: The remains of the arcading in the chapel give an impression of how richly this room was once decorated
Right: A reconstruction of the chapel in the 14th century. The altar would have been located against the south-east wall

view of the altar and any worship taking place from the first floor of the main tower, where the residential apartments were located. A further squint is located slightly higher up the wall. The portcullis, which closed off the entrance to the tower below, would have been raised against the north-west wall.

Originally, the altar would have been set against the south-east wall, lit by two windows with further blind arcading, which is now all gone. Alterations during and after the Civil War changed the appearance of the chapel considerably: the south-east and south-west walls were partly rebuilt and additional floors and a brick stair were inserted, positioned against the south-west wall. The present forebuilding roof dates to the 18th century, when the upper floor was used as a dovecote – its use as a chapel having long since ceased.

8 WALL-WALK

The wall-walk was used by the guards of the tower to observe any potential threats and defend the building. It is currently 60cm lower than it would originally have been, but several of the original paving stones have been left projecting to show the floor level. The positions of the rainwater drains are also visible, although blocked, but one does retain its head-shaped shoot. The parapet wall must have been at least one metre higher than any of the surviving fabric, with only the fishtail-shaped bases of arrowloops surviving on the south and west lobes.

View from the Wall-walk

The wall-walk provides excellent views across the city. To the south is a grassed area in front of the 18th-century court and prison buildings, which was known as the Eye of the Ridings. The three Ridings made up the county of Yorkshire, and elections were held here until 1831. The North Riding's election

Below: An early 18th-century view of the inner bailey or courtyard of the castle from Clifford's Tower. In the centre of the picture is the Debtors' Prison, while the two buildings on either side were replaced in the course of the 18th century by the Female Prison and the Assize Courts

Above: The wall-walk would originally have been higher than it is today. The outer wall contained a large number of arrow slits; the bases of several remain

A view from the wall-walk

A York Minster
B St Mary, Castlegate
C Fairfax House

results continued to be declared here until 1882, and it is now known as the Eye of York. The 18th-century buildings surrounding it replaced the original medieval and post-medieval buildings of the castle.

To the west of the Eye of York are the Assize Courts, built between 1773 and 1777 to the design of John Carr (1723–1807), one of Yorkshire's leading architects and lord mayor of York. To the south is the Debtors' Prison, built as a county gaol, possibly by William Wakefield of Huby (1672–1730), who was later involved in repairs to the castle. The prison was begun in 1701 and completed by 1705, in the English Baroque style. The area in front of the central block, enclosed on either side by the wings, was fenced off and used as an exercise yard for the prisoners. The building, with the former Female Prison, now forms part of the Castle Museum.

The Female Prison was built to reflect the Ionic façade of the Assize Courts. Designed by Thomas Wilkinson and John Prince in 1779, the building was erected between 1780 and 1783 under the supervision of John Carr. The wings flanking the original central block were erected in about 1802 by Peter Atkinson.

Baile Hill and the Outer Bailey

To the west, on the opposite side of the river Ouse, is Baile Hill, the motte of York's second, post-Conquest castle, constructed in 1069 (see map on page 25). When Clifford's Tower and the castle were built in stone in the 13th century, Baile Hill became redundant. The motte of Clifford's Tower was originally surrounded by a ditch filled with water. To the north-east there was an outer bailey, protected by a further large ditch filled with water, and surrounded by a rampart and palisade. The ditch ran beneath what is now the Hilton Hotel and the outer bailey gate was on the line of Castlegate. To the

Left: *A view of Baile Hill, the motte of the second castle, built in 1069. It is now enclosed within the city walls*

Below: *The King's Fishpond or Pool provided a ready source of food. This 15th-century illustration shows a man fishing*

east is the river Foss, which formed part of the defences of the castle. Much of the area beyond the river was part of a large pool of water called the King's Fishpond or Pool, which was formed by damming the river Foss. Fish taken from the pool were often used as gifts to local dignitaries from the king. In 1251, fish from here were served at the wedding banquet of Henry III's eldest daughter.

EXTERIOR
Motte and Drawbridge

The motte on which Clifford's Tower stands is artificial, probably built to support the keep of William the Conqueror's first castle of 1068. Its size and shape have been altered and the present motte is taller than it would have been when it was first built. During underpinning works in 1903, supervised by the engineer Sir Basil Mott (1859–1938), timbers associated with an earlier keep were discovered lying between three and five metres below the current surface. A palisade, or stockade, around the tower was situated on the terrace at the top of the motte, traces of which were found in 1913.

Originally, a stone bridge linked the inner bailey of the castle to Clifford's Tower. It was replaced by a timber drawbridge during the refortification of Clifford's Tower in 1643. The bridge spanned the moat from an entrance in the bailey wall to a flight of steps halfway up the motte, but it was removed in the early 18th century.

Lobes

The design of the tower can be appreciated by walking around the base of the motte. The walls are faced with finely jointed ashlar (square-cut) masonry of local magnesian limestone, but several repairs can be clearly seen. A large crack runs the full height of the south lobe. It was first recorded in 1358, passing through a window at first-floor level. The window was repaired in the 1360s by filling it with masonry, leaving only a narrow opening. Between the west and north lobes is a turret that encloses three latrine shafts. A pair of very small loop openings lights the ground-floor latrines.

The east lobe has distorted badly as a result of subsidence. The motte was surrounded by a moat fed by the river Foss and flooding, reported as early as 1316, contributed to the structural problems.

Remains of the Castle Bailey

The curtain wall of the inner bailey had at least six towers, of which two survive, and two gatehouses. The north gate, or 'Great Gate', was located to the east of Clifford's Tower. Behind the Assize Courts is a section of medieval curtain wall, although much altered. A small postern gate leads through the curtain wall to what was originally an outer enclosure on the west side of the castle, with a further tower and postern gate.

At the rear of the Castle Museum are the south angle and south-east tower. Between the two towers was the south gate. Although it was largely demolished in about 1730 its form is well known and the drawbridge pit and position of the flanking towers can be seen. The position of the gate in the curtain wall is visible as a large rectangular area of reused limestone.

Below: This view of the castle by Francis Place shows the blocked south gate and its flanking towers before their demolition in about 1730

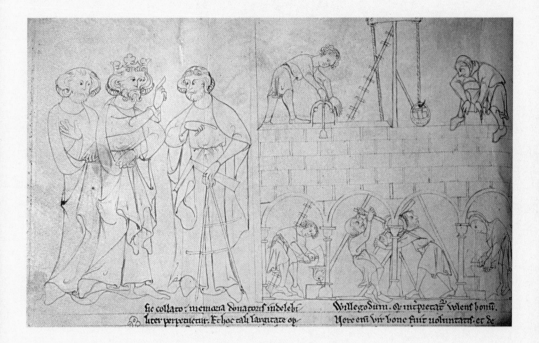

The text beneath the drawing reads:

fic collato: memoria Donatozuf mdelebi
	liter perpetuetur. Et hoc ali laruitate op

Willego Dum. og incipietat wlent bonu.
Yere em vir bone fuit uoluntatif. et de

Master Craftsmen and the Design of Clifford's Tower

The four-lobed design of Clifford's Tower is very unusual and has few precedents. The closest parallels are in France at Amblény, Aisne and Étampes, all in the préfecture of Seine-et-Oise. It has often been suggested that the design for the tower must have originated in France.

The mason Henry de Reyns and the carpenter Simon of Northampton are known to have visited York to advise on the rebuilding of the castle. The early years of Henry de Reyns's career are unclear, but it is possible that he was employed on works at Rheims Cathedral before 1239. He was subsequently involved in the construction of the King's Chapel at Windsor Castle between 1239 and 1243, where he was recorded as master of the king's masons. The year following his visit to York, Henry was engaged in the rebuilding of Westminster Abbey, becoming master of the works on the project. His work at Westminster Abbey shows elements of French design. The rebuilding of the abbey was nearing completion in 1253 but Henry appears to have died, or at least retired, by June of that year.

Simon of Northampton is first recorded as one of the king's five carpenters in 1226. It is not known what he worked on until 1234, when he was repairing the roof of the chamber and chapel at the king's manor at Havering, Essex. From 1236 he spent nearly 15 years at Windsor Castle, where he was in charge of the works.

Henry de Reyns and Simon of Northampton are known to have visited York to advise on the rebuilding of the castle

Above: A mid-13th-century drawing by the chronicler Matthew Paris, showing masons at work on the construction of a tower, possibly meant to represent Clifford's Tower. To the left are craftsmen consulting with the king

History

William the Conqueror
built the first castle at
York in 1068. The motte
on which Clifford's
Tower sits forms part of
this original castle. The
stone tower, which we
now know as Clifford's
Tower, was built during
the reign of Henry III.
It was used as the
king's treasury and
a royal mint.

The tower was
besieged during the
Civil War and soon
afterwards it was
reduced to a shell by
fire. In later years, it
was used as a dovecote
and a prison.

YORK BEFORE 1066

Prehistoric York

Evidence for prehistoric settlement in York is scarce, but occasional finds, including flint tools and hand axes, suggest that people passed through the area. Features of the natural landscape of York formed an early crossroads during the Stone and Bronze Ages. The rivers Ouse and Foss, both probably exploited for river transport, join at York, but the Ouse also crosses a glacial moraine, or raised ridge, which passes across the Vale of York. These features have made York an important strategic place for transport and defence.

Roman York

From AD43 the Romans began their conquest of Britain. Initially the invasion was limited to the south and to the East Midlands, but from AD71 tribal revolts drew the Romans northwards. The Ninth Legion, which had been based in Lincoln, was used for the advance and an earth and timber fortress was erected at York on the north side of the river Ouse. By the second century a *colonia* (a civilian settlement) had been established on the south side of the Ouse. Cemeteries lined the Roman roads into the city and a number of burials have been found in the area later occupied by the medieval castle. Stone coffins or sarcophagi have been found, with inscriptions relating to the Sixth Legion, and also a wooden coffin, containing the skeleton of a young woman buried with bronze and bone bracelets.

Anglian and Viking York

Following the withdrawal of Roman administration in the early fifth century, the region was eventually conquered by the Anglian King Edwin, who was baptized as a Christian in Eoforwic (York) in 627. During this period a settlement was located close to the site of Clifford's Tower, by the confluence of York's two rivers. Anglian finds from the site of Clifford's Tower include clay loom-weights, a bronze hanging bowl, and a bone trial piece incised with interlace decoration. These suggest a substantial settlement engaged in trading activities.

As a major river trading centre, the wealthy city attracted the Vikings, who raided along the east coast from 797 and captured the city in 866, subsequently naming it Jorvic. Excavations in Coppergate have revealed much evidence for the period, with a series of long narrow tenements bounded by Coppergate and the river Foss. The city and region fluctuated between the control of the Vikings and Saxons in the 10th and 11th centuries. In this period the area of the castle was once again used as a cemetery, probably associated with the church of St Mary, Castlegate, which was built before the Norman Conquest.

Above: *An Anglian helmet excavated in Coppergate, York*
Below: *Viking beads, found in York*

Facing page: *A detail of the interior of Clifford's Tower in ruins by J S Prout, 1840*

Above: A 12th-century English manuscript illustration of William the Conqueror riding with his soldiers. William built the first castle at York

Below: York Castle as it might have looked in the late 11th century. The second timber tower on the motte was built in 1070 after its predecessor was destroyed by the Danes

THE NORMAN CASTLE

Soon after the Norman Conquest in 1066 there was a revolt in the North against the invasion. William the Conqueror (r. 1066–87) marched north in the summer of 1068, building a series of castles as he progressed, including one at York. A garrison of 500 men was left at York to guard the new castle, which took the form of a motte and bailey constructed in earth and timber. The motte on which Clifford's Tower sits forms part of this original castle. William returned south, confident that the rebellion had been contained, and establishing further castles at Lincoln, Huntingdon and Cambridge. The revolt, however, was not so easily suppressed. The Norman earl of Northumbria was killed with many of his men at Durham in January 1069, and a force of Northumbrians, under Edgar Ætheling, attacked the city and castle of York. William hurriedly returned to York, catching the Northumbrian forces unaware. Ætheling fled to Scotland and many of the rebels were killed. During William's stay in York, a second castle was started on the western bank of the Ouse, now called the 'Old Baile'. The new castle and its garrisons managed to suppress a further revolt after William had left York in 1069.

York's defences were soon tested by a large Danish fleet, which had already attacked the ports of Dover, Sandwich, Ipswich and Norwich in the autumn of 1069. The fleet sailed up the Humber, joining forces with the Northumbrians before attacking the garrison in York in September 1070. The garrison proceeded to burn the houses around the castle to prevent their timber being used to bridge the castle ditches. The city was also set on fire, either by the garrison or by the Danes. The Norman garrison was eventually overcome by the Danish army

and the castles were destroyed. William immediately returned to York and proceeded to lay waste a belt of the country around the city to the west and north. The Danes retreated down the Humber in the winter and the castles were reconstructed in the same year.

By 1072, York Castle consisted of two mottes on either side of the river Ouse. The one on the west bank, known as the 'Old Baile', consisted of a motte and bailey, while the other one on the east bank consisted of a motte and two baileys, linked by a gate.

Little is known about York Castle for the next 60 years, although some minor works are recorded to the castle in the 1130s. During King Stephen's troubled reign (1135–54), the castle featured briefly in national events. Henry of Anjou (the future Henry II) met his great-uncle David (king of Scotland) and the earl of Chester at Carlisle in 1149, where they planned an attack against Stephen. Stephen heard of the plan and quickly made his way to York with a large army to meet the invasion, which was abandoned when the earl of Chester failed to join forces with his allies.

In the early 1170s, a rebellion against Henry II (r. 1154–89) was instigated by his wife, Queen Eleanor, through her sons and with the aid of Louis, king of France. The crisis triggered some spending on the castle, which included works to the gaol, and more than £15 was spent on the tower, the predecessor of Clifford's Tower, in 1173. During the rebellion William, king of the Scots, had invaded England, but he was captured at Alnwick. The terms of his release made William vassal of the king of England, and after the suppression of the revolt he paid homage to Henry in York.

Above: Henry II shown on horseback on a royal seal. Henry undertook some work at York in 1173, but spent much more money on building the keep at Scarborough Castle, Yorkshire
Below: Iron arrowheads found in York indicate some of the weaponry available in the Norman period

Above: A reconstruction of the horrific events at the castle in March 1190, when the Jews of York were attacked by an angry mob

THE JEWS AND THE MASSACRE OF 1190

The most notorious event in the castle's history took place in 1190. The two most prominent Jews of York, Benedict and Joceus, who were moneylenders to the crusader king Richard I (r.1189–99), attended his coronation in London. Along with others, they became the victims of anti-Semitic riots surrounding the event, which soon spread to other cities. Some were superstitious about Jews being present at a coronation. In addition, the third crusade had led to propaganda not only against the Muslims, but also against the Jews, who were seen as 'infidels' because they did not believe in Jesus. Rumours spread that the king had ordered a massacre of the Jews, although he had done nothing of the kind. Benedict was killed on his way home to York and soon after, in March 1190, the population of York attacked Benedict's house in Coney Street, killing everyone inside. The locals were motivated not just by events in London but also by a more mercenary desire to clear their debts owed to the Jewish moneylenders. Most of the remaining Jews in the city fled to the castle, taking their belongings with them. The constable of the castle, as an employee of the king, granted them protection. They remained in the castle for many days. In the meantime, Joceus's house was also attacked and the inhabitants were killed, and during

The Jews and the Crown

The Norman Conquest first brought a significant number of Jews to England. At that time, Jews were not permitted to own land or to engage in trades or professions. They were limited to lending money for profit, an activity forbidden to Christians, since usury was considered a sin. William I needed to borrow large sums of money to build castles and secure his conquest, so he brought over Jewish merchants from Rouen, Normandy, in 1070, who provided him with a useful source of income.

Under Henry I (r. 1100–35) a royal charter was issued, allowing Jews to move about the country without paying tolls, and to buy and sell goods and property. They had the right to be tried by their peers and to swear on the Torah rather than the Gospels. The Jews were viewed as the king's property. Relations with the Crown were strained during Stephen's reign, particularly after the king burned down the house of a Jew in Oxford because the owner refused to pay a contribution to the king's expenses.

Under Henry II the widespread settlement of Jews enabled the king to borrow money as he required, with repayments made through the sheriffs of the counties. The king benefited enormously from this system of moneylending, since property obtained in this way went to the Crown on the death of the moneylender.

In the latter part of Henry II's reign anti-Semitic sentiment was growing among the upper classes, who owed a lot of money. This anti-Semitism was further inflamed by the crusades and when Richard I went on crusade in 1190, the Jews were open to attack in his absence.

With the accession of Henry III in 1216 initially life became a little easier for the Jews. In the 1230s, however, Jews were gradually expelled from some boroughs. The Jews were finally expelled from England in 1290 by royal edict, and were only formally readmitted in the mid-17th century.

William I brought over Jewish merchants from Rouen, Normandy, who provided him with money to secure his conquest

Left: A Jewish wizard is shown introducing Theophilus, a sixth-century cleric, to the devil, in an illustration from the Lambeth Apocalypse, of about 1260. Jews were often portrayed in an anti-Semitic way, with exaggerated features

the days which followed, any Jews found outside the castle walls were either forcibly baptized or killed.

While the Jews sheltered in the castle, the constable was called away on business. On his return, the Jews were afraid that they would be betrayed, so they refused to let the constable back in. The constable consequently went to the sheriff, who summoned troops to the castle, where they were joined by a large mob from York and the surrounding area. The Jews attempted to stave off the attack of the mob by pulling stones out of the wall of the interior of the tower and throwing them at their attackers.

After a long siege, a number of the Jews realized that they would not be let out alive, and so they decided to take their own lives, rather than be killed by the mob. The various sources are not completely clear about the sequence of events, but it seems that on the eve of the Jewish Sabbath, 16 March (which fell on the Friday before Palm Sunday), the father of each family allegedly killed his wife and children and set fire to their belongings and to the castle. The few who had not wished to take their own lives, and who survived the fire, were killed by the mob the following morning when they left the castle, under assurances of safe passage from Richard Malebisse, the leader of the mob. The mob then demanded access to York Minster, where the Jews had deposited accounts of local debts, and they burned the documents.

The number of Jews involved is still disputed. It is currently thought that there were approximately 150 Jews in the castle, representing between 20 and 40 families. Other estimates over the centuries have put the numbers higher.

The castle was repaired and the tower rebuilt soon after the horrific event. The work was completed in 1193 at a total cost of nearly £236, which was a considerable sum at the time.

KING JOHN

During John's reign (1199–1216) small but regular expenditure was made to maintain and improve the castle. Following John's visit to York in March 1200, a programme of works recorded in the pipe rolls (annual exchequer accounts) suggests that at

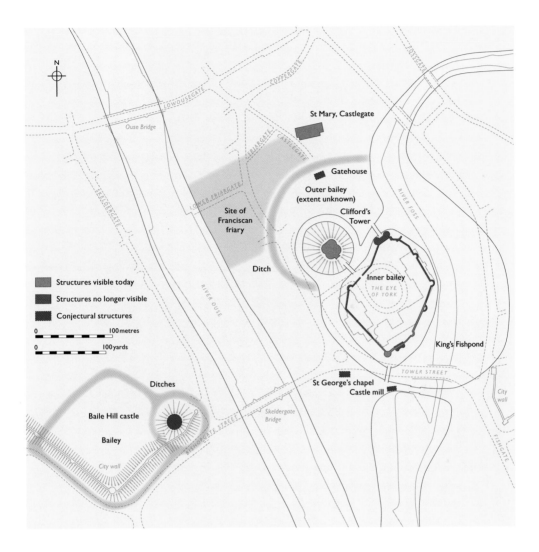

Above: York Castle in about 1275, showing the former extent of the moats and areas of water

least part of the castle was being rebuilt in stone, including repairs to the castle bridge linking Clifford's Tower to the bailey. John's visit had not been entirely harmonious, as the citizens of York angered the king by not greeting him on his arrival. For this act of disloyalty, they were fined £100.

When John visited York in 1204, the sheriff was ordered to collect as much stone and lime as possible for strengthening the castle, spending nearly £15. Some of this work appears to have included building the south gatehouse and the drawbridge pit, as well as sections of the curtain wall. The gaol was in need of constant repair throughout John's reign and it is recorded that irons were bought for prisoners at a cost of £4 5s.

THE CONSTRUCTION OF CLIFFORD'S TOWER AND REBUILDING THE CASTLE

During the early years of Henry III's reign (1216–72) at least one large building project was undertaken at York: a house was built in front of the gaol for the king between 1237 and 1238. Although some buildings were made of stone, some of the fortifications were still timber; supplies were obtained in 1225

Right: The distinctive magnesian limestone used for rebuilding the castle was obtained from Tadcaster in Yorkshire. In this early 14th-century manuscript illustration masons are at work shaping and laying stone with which they have been provided
Below: Henry III (r.1216–72) being crowned. Henry's long reign saw York Castle almost entirely rebuilt

to repair the bridge, houses and 'breaches in stockade of the castle'. In 1228, some of the timber work had been blown down by a 'great wind', including the castle gate.

The king's visit to York in 1244 prompted the rebuilding of the castle. The possibility of war with Scotland loomed, so the sheriff was instructed to obtain materials and timber for strengthening the castle's defences in August 1244. After the Scottish crisis had passed, this temporary measure was abandoned in favour of a complete reconstruction. The king clearly envisaged an ambitious project, for in March 1245 he sent master Simon the carpenter and master Henry the mason to York (see page 17). They were to survey the castle to see how it should best be rebuilt and advise the sheriff.

Building began in 1246 with annual allowances made of between £133 and £267 (about £71,000 and £142,000 at current values). Some of the old castle buildings, including the gaol and a chapel, were demolished to make way for replacements. By 1250, some of the towers on the inner bailey curtain wall were nearing completion, with oaks being obtained for the making of roof boards and lead (to cover the roofs) ordered from Derbyshire. Work on Clifford's Tower, known at the time as the King's Tower, is not recorded until 1251. In September, the sheriff of York received, and had to guard, 20 cartloads of lead from the bailiff of the Peak (Derbyshire), for works on the castle, while the following day, orders were issued for 20 oaks.

In November 1251, the castle was being prepared to receive the king. Master Richard, the king's cook, was using carpenters to build the castle mill and other necessities so that the castle would be ready for the king's visit. Between 1252 and 1253 at least 80 oaks were used for building works and parts of the castle were being roofed the following year.

The speed of work and the expenditure on the castle show signs of slowing from the start of 1256, with 100 marks (equivalent to £66) being allocated annually on finishing the castle. Work was clearly not proceeding as quickly as expected and in 1257 Roger Thurkelby, a justice in eyre (a court of itinerant justices), was ordered to go to the castle with the sheriff to establish how much needed to be done and at what cost. There is a note of exasperation in this order, as the king had told the sheriff to finish the castle on several occasions, but the sheriff, so the king was informed, had made little effort to do so. Roger's visit must have had some effect, as money was spent on roofing the castle the following year and some parts of the castle had finally been completed, including the king's chapel. Progress continued to be slow and it is not until 1262 that the castle appears to have been largely completed as originally envisaged 17 years earlier. The total cost of rebuilding the castle in Henry III's reign exceeded £3,700 – a considerable sum of money in the 13th century and over £2 million at current values.

Above: Peveril, or Peak, Castle was the royal administrative centre of the Peak District – the source of lead to cover the roofs of York Castle

Below: A scene in a counting house, showing men taking money from a chest, from a 14th-century Italian manuscript. Clifford's Tower was used as a treasury at this time

YORK CASTLE IN THE LATER MIDDLE AGES
Exchequer, Treasury and Residence

During the course of the 14th century, the castle became the principal northern base of the Crown, and played an important role in operations against Scotland. In 1298 the king's exchequer was established in the castle and Clifford's Tower prepared for the treasury of receipt, which involved storing money to pay for the war and receiving taxes. Some

Above: Edward II being created prince of Wales in 1301 by his father, Edward I, from an early 14th-century English manuscript. Several improvements were made to the castle during Edward II's reign

modifications to the building were needed, including new doors, locks and 'other things which are lacking for the safeguarding of our treasury which we shall place there'. The royal courts, treasury and exchequer were evidently transferred from London to York on a number of occasions until 1392, and on each occasion, extensive references are made to their provision. In 1304, houses in the castle in which Parliament sat were repaired and chests were obtained for storing documents and other items relating to the exchequer.

Edward II (r. 1307–27) had a troubled reign, exacerbated by his weakness for appointing personal favourites to positions of authority. In 1312 the barons executed Piers Gaveston, Edward's favourite at the time. During Edward's subsequent stay in York, several improvements were made to the castle: a roof was constructed for the chapel, which had recently been built inside Clifford's Tower, and a further tower and outwork were built, which used to stand to the south-west of the castle until 1807.

By 1320, Edward II had replaced Gaveston as a royal favourite with Sir Hugh Despenser and his son. Their influence over the king prompted the barons to rebel again, led by the earl of Lancaster. The warring parties met at Boroughbridge in Aldborough, Yorkshire, in March 1322, where the rebels were captured. Lancaster was executed at Pontefract Castle and buried at Pontefract Priory, but his fellow rebel, Lord Roger de Clifford, was hung in chains from Clifford's Tower.

When the exchequer and other state offices left York in 1322, a number of items of furniture were left in Clifford's Tower, including a large counter, which measured 11ft by 3ft (3.4m by 0.9m), a screen, barriers and bench seats. In 1327 the exchequer was again moved to York 'so long as the king shall stay there for the expedition of the Scotch war in the north', and houses in the castle were repaired to receive it. At the same time a gate tower within the castle was undergoing refurbishment in order to accommodate the exchequer of the queen mother, Isabella. This included repairing the lead roof and walls and plastering a room over the entrance. In the same year, provision was made to improve the service areas of the castle, with 4 shillings being paid for a hundred wattling rods for making the partitions and spaces in the cellar where the king's wines were kept.

In 1333 a new building was constructed on the north side of the castle for the receipt and exchequers of Queen Philippa (the castle already housed the king's receipt and exchequer). The new building would have been situated towards the north gate. On occasion, Clifford's Tower was used as a residence for important people. In 1338 the houses in the tower were used by the countess of Buchan and her children because her husband was to accompany the king 'to parts beyond the sea ... provided that the king's things in that tower be safely kept for his use'.

Below: The castle as it might have appeared in the early 14th century. The tower and outworks in the foreground were added in 1312

Right: The flooding of the rivers Ouse and Foss has continued to be a problem, as this photograph from the 1970s shows

Below: Repairs to Clifford's Tower were needed soon after it was completed. In this 13th-century French manuscript illustration workmen are shown busy at a variety of tasks on a tall tower

Facing page: The east lobe of the tower, showing the crack running from top to bottom, which was first recorded in 1312

Problems with the Tower

Much of the medieval castle was originally surrounded by the rivers Ouse and Foss and flooding has been a persistent problem. In the winter of 1315 flooding caused the collapse of a large section of curtain wall and softened the motte. Repairs were put in hand, including work to the well inside Clifford's Tower. Numerous further repairs were undertaken during the 1320s; new lead was needed for the houses within the tower in 1323, and the wooden fence around the tower also had to be mended. In 1325, the walls between the tower and castle, which enclosed the approach up the motte, were in need of repair.

Reports on the condition of Clifford's Tower from 1358 and 1360 indicate that the building was showing serious signs of subsidence, a problem noted more than 40 years earlier. The tower had cracked in two places from top to bottom with a quarter of the tower, the east lobe, almost falling over. It was suggested that the only solution was to pull it down and rebuild it at a cost of more than 200 marks. The buildings inside the tower were also in poor condition, with the lead from the roofs either removed or damaged, the timber decayed and ironwork removed from the doorways and gates.

The survey of the castle of 1360 also suggests that it was in an extremely poor state of repair. The vaulted passage of the 'great gate', a two-storey structure, was cracked, while the room above was uninhabitable. Part of a tower in the western corner of the inner bailey had fallen into the castle ditch, while the wall of a tower called 'le Boretour' was split right through and half collapsed. The foundations of the castle gaol were in poor condition due to flooding and the dungeon was unuseable. Most of the buildings within the bailey, including the chapel, exchequer and halls, were either in a very poor state of repair or were in ruins. At the time it was unlikely that the castle could have resisted an attack.

As a result, the castle was completely renovated between 1360 and 1365, with over £800 being spent. In 1362, iron stays were installed to support a bretesse, a covered timber gallery on the wall-head of the tower, while a glazier fitted 32 square feet of glass in the windows in the chapel above the entrance.

In 1364, wall tiles were bought for the kitchen chimneys and the chapel screen, and there is also a record of two great stones being bought for the mantelpieces. In 1365, 40 stone (254kg) of lead sheet was bought for re-roofing the turret beside the chapel and for the kitchen gutters and 'evesplates'. The banks of the river Foss were strengthened with straw and rammed earth, presumably in an attempt to prevent the frequent flooding of the castle.

During the 15th century, minor repairs are recorded to the great hall, but from 1484 Richard III (r.1483–5) intended to rebuild the castle completely. Work on the castle appears to have stopped on the death of Richard III at the battle of Bosworth in 1485. In 1487, the mayor of York told the new king, Henry VII (r.1485–1509), that the city was decayed due to the 'takyng downe of yowe castell there by King Richard and as yet not re-edified'.

CLIFFORD'S TOWER IN THE 16TH AND 17TH CENTURIES

For the first half of the 16th century, the tower – sometimes called the 'arx' or 'citadel' – appears to have been little used, although it was occasionally pressed into service as a venue for public events, such as executions. The fabric of the castle site was evidently in decline. Writing in 1540, the antiquary John Leland described the castle as a desolate ruin. Shortly after Leland's observations, some repairs and improvements were made in the 1540s, particularly to the gaol.

Attempted Demolition

The last decade of the 16th century saw one of the greatest threats to the survival of Clifford's Tower. By 1596 the tower was unused, but it emerged that the gaoler, Robert Redhead, was gradually dismantling the topmost section of the tower and a flanking wall in order to obtain stone and lime for the erection of a cockpit in the city. Locals were up in arms: the aldermen and mayor of York raised a petition to the Crown against the demolition and Redhead was informed that he must stop.

This was not the end of the matter, however, and in October 1596 rumours were once again circulating that Redhead and his accomplices had, under the pretence of using some of the stone for legitimate repairs to other buildings in the castle, once again intended to make some money by selling some of the stone for lime-burning. By December 1597, Redhead's workmen were seen on the top of the tower,

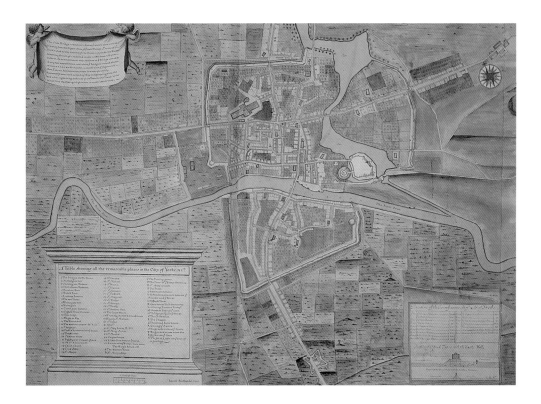

throwing stones from the parapet and rolling them down the motte. The Corporation of York claimed that Redhead intended to weaken the tower by picking stonework out from the interior and to undermine it by the use of rabbits! It is clear that Redhead was prevented, by some means, from continuing his demolition work.

This is the first time that the name 'Clifford's Tower' is recorded. Previously, the tower had been known as the King's Tower or the Great Tower. The name appears to be a local one – a reference either to the hanging of Roger de Clifford's body from the tower in 1322 or to the role of the Clifford family as constables of the castle.

Civil War

James I (r.1603–25) sold many ruined properties to raise funds. Clifford's Tower was granted by the Crown to Edmund Duffield and John Babbington in 1614. The tower then passed through various owners, none of whom appears to have used it, until the outbreak of the Civil War in August 1642. In September the earl of Cumberland was appointed lieutenant-general of the royalist forces in the North. The king asked him to prepare the city against attack, with guns mounted on the city gates. Clifford's Tower, however, was not repaired until after Queen Henrietta Maria arrived in York in March 1643. The queen had been in Holland raising money and collecting arms for the king and she was forced to land at Bridlington, to the east of York, to avoid the parliamentarian forces. New timbers were laid on the walls in Clifford's Tower, rooms were provided for stores,

Above: A plan of York prepared by the surveyor Jacob Richards in 1682. The inner bailey and Clifford's Tower are still surrounded by their water defences at this time

Below: A portrait of Queen Henrietta Maria, wife of Charles I, after Sir Anthony Van Dyck, about 1632–5. Her efforts saw Clifford's Tower refortified for the royalist cause

Above: A portrait of Henry Clifford, 5th earl of Cumberland, by Daniel Mytens. He was one of the constables of the castle in the 17th century and his coat of arms is on the forebuilding

Below: A portrait of Prince Rupert, attributed to Gerrit van Honthorst, about 1641–2. He led the royalist forces at the battle of Marston Moor in 1643. The defeat of Rupert triggered the final stage of the parliamentarian siege of York and Clifford's Tower

the forebuilding was rebuilt with the royal coat of arms and a deeper moat was dug with a drawbridge and palisades. Cannon brought by the queen from Holland were mounted on a platform on top of the tower. Colonel Sir Francis John Cobb was made governor of the tower and remained there throughout the subsequent siege. The queen left York in June 1643, taking 4,500 men and weapons to reinforce the king's army at Oxford.

The conflict reached York after the northern royalist army, led by the earl of Newcastle, retreated from Durham to York on 16 April 1644. The royalists were closely followed by Scottish armies, who joined up with the parliamentarians under Fairfax at Tadcaster. By 23 April, the city was under siege by these combined troops, who made several unsuccessful attempts to storm the gates and undermine the walls. A report from the parliamentarian side on 4 June mentioned the cannon on Clifford's Tower firing frequently on their men, although with no loss of life. The following day it was reported that a battery placed on a hill near Walmgate had continued the attack on the castle and the city, with Clifford's Tower returning heavy fire. From the royalist side came a report that:

> When the enemy advanced with their whole cannon (which carried a 60-pound bullet) from Gate-Foulford, to plant it on Heslington Hill; the Lieutenant Collonell of the tower [Clifford's Tower], being then upon the platforme, commanded David Guillome, a loyall citizen, the cannoneers mate, to travers the guns, and to levell them according to art, and giving fire to a demy culveren, did that execution, which made the enemy run all from their cannon, where she lay all that day betwixt Foulford and York.

The parliamentarian cannon, mentioned in the report, was known as the Queen's Pocket Pistol. It had been captured from the earl of Newcastle at Hull in 1643 and was responsible, a day later, for making a breach in Clifford's Tower.

Negotiations between the two sides broke down and the subsequent arrival of Prince Rupert with a relieving royalist army led the parliamentarians to raise the siege on 30 June and concentrate their forces on Marston Moor. Their victory in that battle on 3 July caused the royalists to flee and the siege to be renewed. The city finally surrendered on 16 July and the garrisons were allowed to march out with full honour, to be replaced by parliamentarian soldiers. The damage inflicted on the city had been extensive, with most of the suburbs of the city destroyed by fire and buildings within the walls wrecked by cannon.

In 1646, the House of Commons decided that Clifford's Tower should be kept garrisoned, although the city garrison

was dismantled the following year. When Cromwell rode into York in 1650, the event was celebrated with a salute of cannon fire from the tower.

The tower seems to have been used mainly as an armoury in this period, with cannon and 3,000 muskets being transported from there in 1650 and 1652. In 1662, it is recorded that the tower was to be used as a magazine, with Major Scott in command of the 40 men. The tower remained in much the same state until 1684.

The Destruction of Clifford's Tower

In 1683 a survey of Clifford's Tower and the castle was undertaken to assess its defensive capabilities. It was recommended that the tower should be de-garrisoned, which would save several hundred pounds and make troops available for a more valuable posting, and that it should perhaps be demolished. This solution would have been popular with many of York's citizens, who drunk toasts 'to the demolition of the Minced Pie', a derisive name for the tower.

Events overtook the report on St George's Day, 23 April 1684, when a gun salute was fired from the top of the tower and Clifford's Tower was reduced by fire to a shell. The tower was left standing, but damaged; the shell was used for storage and a guard was maintained on the door until 1690. Cannon were still kept there and in 1687 a gunner was blown from the top of the tower while discharging 'one of the great gunns'; he later died from his injuries. In 1688, the birthday of James II (r.1685–9) was celebrated with a salute of the 'great gunns'. The tower continued to be held by the Crown until 1699, when it was returned to the freeholder, Lady Suzanna Thompson, who subsequently sold the property to Richard Sowray, a resident of York.

Above: An engraving by W H Toms after a drawing by Francis Place of Clifford's Tower in 1680, before it was blown up in 1684
Below: The Queen's Pocket Pistol, the parliamentarian cannon which was used to blow a hole in Clifford's Tower, which is now at Dover Castle

Above: A portrait of the architect John Carr by Sir William Beechey, 1791. Carr designed the new Assize Courts and was lord mayor of York
Below: Clifford's Tower and its motte had become a garden feature in Samuel Waud's house by the time of this print of 1730. The Waud residence is to the right of the tower

CLIFFORD'S TOWER IN THE 18TH CENTURY

Clifford's Tower passed through various hands until it was acquired by Samuel Waud, a local gentleman, in 1727. The tower stayed in the Waud family for three generations until 1825. Waud added a mansion shortly after 1727 on the east side of the motte, and the tower became a folly in the garden.

The 18th century saw much development in the remainder of the castle. Until then, prisoners were still housed in the towers on the curtain wall of the inner bailey. The towers had been built in the 13th century and were principally intended for defence, but by the 14th century they had been pressed into service as additional accommodation for prisoners. Between 1701 and 1705, the County Gaol (now known as the Debtors' Prison) was built, possibly designed by William Wakefield. From the front, the right wing housed the debtors, the governor and the gaoler, and the left housed the felons and the chapel. In 1708, some of the towers of the castle were demolished and in 1731 the wet ditch on the west side was drained.

Between 1773 and 1777 the new Assize Courts were built, designed by John Carr to replace the Grand Jury House on the west side of the bailey. The Assize Courts were originally smaller, encompassing only the central section of the current building; extensions were added to each end in 1818 and to the rear of the building between 1821 and 1823. Between 1780 and 1783 the Female Prison was built, replacing the old Moot Hall, a meeting hall on the eastern side of the bailey. Originally built to match the Assize Courts, the prison was designed by Thomas Wilkinson and John Prince, but John Carr oversaw the building work. The Female Prison was also extended in about 1802 when wings were added and the rear courtyard was enclosed with walls.

By 1790, the central area of the castle yard – an oval lawn – was known as the Eye of the Ridings. It was the location for county elections for Yorkshire until 1831 and North Riding election results were declared here until 1882. In 1802, the

Prisoners at York Castle

The castle provided accommodation not only for guests, but also for some well-known prisoners. In 1307, the earl of Strathearn was held at the castle, accompanied by six attendants, all of whom were accommodated at the earl's expense. This relatively luxurious treatment contrasts with that of Robert Aske, a rebel and leader of the Pilgrimage of Grace in 1536, a popular rising in Yorkshire against the break with Rome and the Suppression of the monasteries. In 1537 Aske was held at York Castle; records relate that his 'execution shall be done on the height of the castle dungeon where the sheriffs of the city have no authority' and his body was duly hung from the tower.

George Fox, founder of the Society of Friends, and William Dewsbury, a fellow Quaker, were both held at the tower. Fox was imprisoned here for two nights while on his way to Scarborough Castle in 1665 after four years of incarceration at Dewsbury.

One of the most notorious prisoners held at the castle was the highwayman Dick Turpin (1705–39). Working under the alias of John Palmer, Turpin set himself up as a horse trader. His criminal career had started with deer theft, before progressing to burglary, horse theft and murder. While he was staying at a Yorkshire inn, the local magistrates became suspicious of how 'Palmer' made his money and he was arrested. Imprisoned at York Castle, he sent a letter to his brother-in-law which was intercepted, and his true identity was revealed by his handwriting. Turpin was subsequently found guilty of several counts of horse theft and executed on 7 April 1739 at the Knavesmire, York.

> Imprisoned at York Castle, Dick Turpin sent a letter to his brother-in-law which was intercepted, and his true identity was revealed by his handwriting

Above: An 18th-century print of Dick Turpin shooting Tom King, in an imaginative recreation of one of his crimes

Above: A 19th-century engraving of
an execution taking place outside
the castle walls

Below: Clifford's Tower by F Bedford,
1841, shortly after the prison was
built. The tower's motte has been cut
back and a stone wall built around it
in order to create more space

place of execution was moved from York Tyburn on the
Knavesmire to the New Drop, to the back of the new Assize
Courts outside the castle walls. A small access door from the
castle interior survives. It was used until 1868, when executions
were carried out inside the prison walls at the north end of
the Female Prison. Executions finally stopped in 1896.

THE CASTLE IN THE 19TH CENTURY

During the 19th century there was pressure to improve prison
buildings because of stricter regulations about living conditions
for prisoners. In 1824 the prison was enlarged, and in the
following year Waud's property was bought to provide
additional land. In 1824 three designs were prepared for
improving the prison. Robert Wallace proposed to build
corridors radiating out to an outer wall from Clifford's Tower
itself, which was to be used as a chapel and kitchen. The
winning design by P F Robinson and G T Andrews was similar
to Wallace's but included a completely new building – a round
governor's house with the prison blocks leading from it,
positioned to the north-east of Clifford's Tower, with a large
outer wall and a new gatehouse on the north-west corner.
This meant that Waud's house had to be demolished, along
with the old north gate, Castlegate postern and the houses
on the east side of Castlegate.

Building work began in 1826 and was completed in 1835.
The dark gritstone which was used to build the 10m-high
battlemented outer wall and towering gatehouse had a sombre
effect on the streets skirting the prison. In order to build a road
that led from the gatehouse round Clifford's Tower to the new
prison, it was necessary to cut away the base of the motte and
build a high retaining wall around it. After the prison was built,
public access to Clifford's Tower was limited.

Considerable repair work was carried out to the tower in the late 19th century, including the insertion of iron tie rods into the forebuilding in an attempt to bond it with the main body of the tower. By the turn of the century, the tower was probably at the highest risk of collapse in its history.

THE CASTLE IN THE 20TH CENTURY

In 1900, the castle became a military rather than a civil prison, and the poor structural condition of Clifford's Tower became apparent. A report of 1901 by the Prison Commission revealed that the forebuilding and east lobe were rapidly sinking as the motte beneath them collapsed and the forebuilding was found to have moved away from the tower. The tower was returned to the city of York in August 1902, on the understanding that it would be repaired. A decision was taken to underpin the tower and the engineer Sir Basil Mott was engaged to supervise the work. The south-east section of the tower was underpinned with concrete and five large flying buttresses were inserted into the motte below, linking the retaining wall to the new underpinned foundations. Archaeological observations were made as the work progressed and reported upon in 1903. A layer of burnt timber was examined and thought to date either from the revolt of 1069 or from the destruction of the tower by fire in 1190.

In 1915 the monument was placed in the guardianship of the Office of Works. Access, however, was complicated by the continued presence of the military prison, especially from 1914, when German prisoners of war were kept here. A detailed structural survey was carried out by the Office of Works in

Above: Clifford's Tower is one of the most iconic buildings of York. This painting by L S Lowry of 1959 shows the tower after the prison had been demolished

Below: The main entrance to the prison before it was demolished in the 1930s

1914 and extensive work was recommended. No action was taken at the site during the First World War but in 1919 extensive repairs were finally carried out. The masonry was reinforced with a series of metal rods inserted into the lobe walls, supported by reinforced concrete beams and faced with stone. The rods in each lobe were hooked together to link the entire circumference of the tower, strengthening the support for the walls. The major tears in the stonework were rebuilt with sandstone and the smaller fractures were grouted.

The Office of Works was again active in the castle area in 1924, when it undertook an archaeological investigation on the site of the south gate. The footings of the gate were cleared to the level at which they stand today, revealing the gatehouse (with the blocked gateway) and the 12ft- (3.7m) deep drawbridge pit in front. A large mass of masonry was moved during the excavation, possibly including the support for the drawbridge that would have spanned the moat.

In 1929 the prison was closed and five years later the buildings were sold to the city of York for £8,000. A scheme was approved to demolish all the buildings erected after 1824, including the outer walls and gatehouse of the prison, and the original profile of the motte was restored. The route up the motte from the south-west was removed and a new flight of steps directly up to the forebuilding was constructed. The work was completed by 1936.

Some remnants from the demolished prison survive: an iron-bound gate and the royal arms from the gatehouse are displayed in the Castle Museum, while the fireplace and panelling from the courthouse within the same building are in the Mason's Arms public house in Fishergate.